Why Doesn't God Fix It?

Shining Eternal Light on the Darkness of Chronic Illness

Companion Bible Study

KIMBERLY RAE

Library of Congress Cataloging-in-Publication Data
Rae, Kimberly.
Why Doesn't God Fix It? - Bible Study Companion Booklet/ Kimberly Rae 1st ed.
Sick & Tired Series

Unless otherwise noted, all Scripture taken from the New King James version of the Holy Bible.

First Edition, September 2014
Second Edition, September 2015

ISBN-13: 978-1502309440
ISBN-10: 1502309440

Chapter by Chapter
Bible Study

for Groups or Individuals:

CONTENTS

Chapter One:

Bribing God

. . . if you're feeling like Job, check out who God really is. If you're feeling like Elijah, let yourself be taken care of for awhile. Stop analyzing your feelings and instead get your body the rest and nourishment it needs. If you feel like David, write or say your feelings, but then conclude them with truth. If you feel like Sarah, don't do whatever it is you're thinking of doing! Don't try to bribe, negotiate or threaten God. It doesn't work.

Most of all, like Jesus, test all things, even feelings and temptations, according to the Scriptures, and end your prayers asking that God's will be done. Hold fast to that which is true and reject what is not.

No matter how dark or desperate your feelings are, take them straight to God. He's the only one strong enough to hold them, so let Him have them every time they come . . .

1. But he himself [Elijah] went a day's journey into the wilderness, and came and sat down under a broom tree. And he prayed that he might die, and said, "It is enough! Now, LORD, take my life, for I am no better than my fathers!" 1 Kings 19:4

Elijah had just had an amazing success of faith, a faith and connection to God many of us would envy. Yet he felt a failure when fear took hold and wished to die. Would you consider this a pity party, a struggle with legitimate fears, or a true spiritual failure?

If Elijah had expected a great revival after Mt. Carmel, and was surprised and confused when, instead of his hopes realized, he was threatened by a wicked leader still ruling, could such unfulfilled expectations have caused or contributed to his despair? Can you think of a time in your illness when you expected a hopeful result and were deeply disappointed? Did you feel like Elijah, and perhaps respond to God like him as well?

2. Then as he lay and slept under a broom tree, suddenly an angel touched him, and said to him, "Arise and eat." Then he looked, and there by his head was a cake baked on coals, and a jar of water. So he ate and drank, and lay down again. And the angel of the LORD came back the second time, and touched him, and said, "Arise and eat, because the journey is too great for you." So he arose, and ate and drank; and he went in the strength of that food forty days and forty nights as far as Horeb, the mountain of God. 1 Kings 19:5-8

Does it surprise you how God responded? He did not speak to Elijah at all, but sent a messenger to feed and encourage him. What do you think this tells us about God? What do you think it should mean to us next time we are feeling the way Elijah did?

3. And there he went into a cave, and spent the night in that place; and behold, the word of the LORD came to him, and He said to him, "What are you doing here, Elijah?" So he said, "I have been very zealous for the LORD God of hosts; for the children of Israel have forsaken Your covenant, torn down Your altars, and killed Your prophets with the sword. I alone am left; and they seek to take my life." 1 Kings 19:9-10

Are you shocked at how Elijah speaks to God? Do you think Elijah was wrong to speak this way? Have you ever spoken so openly to God about how you feel? Would you expect such a prayer to make God angry, disappointed, or _____? Why?

4. Then He said, "Go out, and stand on the mountain before the LORD." And behold, the LORD passed by, and a great and strong wind tore into the mountains and broke the rocks in pieces before the LORD, but the LORD was not in the wind; and after the wind an earthquake, but the LORD was not in the earthquake; and after the earthquake a fire, but the LORD was not in the fire; and after the fire a still small voice. 1 Kings 19:11-12

Again, did God surprise you? Would it seem more likely that God would have spoken through the powerful wind or the harsh earthquake or the frightening fire? Why do you think God chose to be in the still small voice? What do you think that means for us?

5. Then the LORD said to him: "Go, return on your way….And Elisha the son of Shaphat of Abel Meholah you shall anoint as prophet in your place….Yet I have reserved seven thousand in Israel, all whose knees have not bowed to Baal. 1 Kings 19:15-18

God sends the discouraged prophet to anoint a man who will work alongside him and be a companion for him. Then God ends the conversation telling Elijah he is not the only one, but rather he is one of seven thousand. What an encouragement! Again, what do these choices from God teach us about God's character toward His servants? Will this change the way you talk to God in the future, or in the way you listen for His answer?

7. For He has not despised nor abhorred the affliction of the afflicted; nor has He hidden His face from him; but when he cried to Him, He heard. Psalm 22:24

What does this verse mean to you? If you put your name in that verse, that "He has not despised nor abhorred the affliction of _____, nor has He hidden His face from _____, but when _____ cried unto Him, He heard," what would this mean for your life right now?

8. Those who seek Him will praise the LORD. Psalm 22:26

When we focus on ourselves and our feelings, is it easy or hard to praise the Lord? How do you think seeking God results in praising Him? Would praising the Lord perhaps change our focus, and perhaps our feelings, too?

Notes:

Chapter Two:

The Feelings of Our Infirmities

. . . If you have chronic health problems, when you're having a flare-up or are in deep pain, you are not likely struggling with temptations toward acts of sin like stealing or gossiping or lust (though I am tempted toward gluttony as my steroids make me VERY hungry). The temptations are inward ones. To fear, to worry, to give in to anxiety or anger or even bitterness. The temptation to envy people who are healthy.

Jesus says He understands. He knows what it is like to feel physical fatigue and pain, much more so than you or I ever will, and all the inward temptations that come with it. He was tempted to fear, to worry, even to envy. Yet He did not sin.

Because He knows, and yet did not sin, He can teach us how to face these temptations without sin as well.

If you have felt burdened down by the feelings that attack you when you are sick or in pain, be encouraged. Jesus understands how you feel. He's been there. He knows what it is like to face the feelings of infirmities. If you let Him, He will face yours with you, praying for you all the way . . .

1. Whoever has no rule over his own spirit is like a city broken down, without walls. Proverbs 25:28

Have you ever felt your emotions turned you into a city broken down and without walls? Describe those times when you feel most vulnerable to attack.

2. He who trusts in his own heart is a fool. Proverbs 28:26

Has following your emotions ever led you into foolishness or sin? Have you done or said things in emotion that you later regretted? Why do you think God says we are fools if we trust our hearts?

3. The heart is deceitful above all things, and desperately wicked; who can know it? Jeremiah 17:9

Have your feelings ever deceived you? Are there certain times, medicines, symptoms that affect your emotions in a way you wish they wouldn't?

4. What does it profit, my brethren, if someone says he has faith but does not have works? Can faith save him? If a brother or sister is naked and destitute of daily food, and one of you says to them, "Depart in peace, be warmed and filled," but you do not give them the things which are needed for the body, what does it profit? Thus also faith by itself, if it does not have works, is dead. James 2:14-17

Do these verses describe faith as a feeling or an action or both? How do you need faith in regard to your illness? How would faith affect your feelings? How would it affect your actions?

5. You number my wanderings; put my tears into Your bottle; are they not in Your book? Psalm 56:8

Having a good cry sometimes helps and we can move on, wiping our tears away. What does it mean to you to think of God keeping your tears in a book and in a bottle? What does that say about how often He is with you, and how much He cares?

6. And God will wipe away every tear from their eyes; there shall be no more death, nor sorrow, nor crying. There shall be no more pain, for the former things have passed away. Revelation 21:4

One day a bottle or book won't be needed for our tears, for God will wipe them all away forever. Did God promise to do that here in this life? When is the promise for? Who is it for?

7. For we have not an high priest which cannot be touched with the feeling of our infirmities; but was in all points tempted like as we are, yet without sin. Hebrews 4:15 KJV

How does it feel to have God tell you that Jesus knows not only your infirmities, but the feelings of them as well? Had you ever thought of that before? Does that change the way you think about approaching God in prayer, or what you pray about?

8. *Who is he who condemns? It is Christ who died, and furthermore is also risen, who is even at the right hand of God, who also makes intercession for us. Romans 8:34*

What are some reasons one person might intercede for another person? Why do you think Jesus intercedes for you? How do you feel about the idea of Jesus praying for you? What do you think He prays for regarding you?

9. *For whatever is born of God overcomes the world. And this is the victory that has overcome the world—our faith. 1 John 5:4*

How can this verse help us face our illness, and even those who believe our illness means a lack of faith?

Notes:

Chapter Three:

Not Enough Faith?

. . . Jesus cares about my suffering and yours. Though He has allowed it for some reason, He hurts with us and He wants to use us to show Himself to the world. Yes, sometimes sickness is a result of sin and dealing with the sin releases people from the sickness it caused. Also yes, sometimes God provides miraculous healing and gets glory through that. However, sometimes He allows sickness to remain because He has a different plan, one that isn't clear to others and often ourselves, but if we trust Him—if we keep the faith others think we do not have—we will one day see how He is being glorified and will be glorified through us and our pain. In the end, our level of faith isn't about something that others can tangibly grasp, measurable by our health or wealth or abilities. Faith is something only God can measure, and what does reveal our faith to others, according to the Scriptures, are our works for Him (James 2:14-17), and some days our greatest work of faith may be enduring hardship as a good soldier of Jesus Christ (2 Timothy 2:3). Other days it may be responding in grace to those people who tell us we're sick because we don't have enough faith (Rom. 12:14).

I don't know how God plans to use my sickness or your sickness, but the how doesn't matter. Just knowing that illness can be part of His plan—rather than because of my lack of faith—gives me, and hopefully you, great comfort today . . .

1. Judge not, that you be not judged. For with what judgment you judge, you will be judged; and with the measure you use, it will be measured back to you. Matthew 7:1-2

If someone is judging us, should we make that a problem between them and us, or leave it as a problem between them and God?

2. For he who eats and drinks in an unworthy manner eats and drinks judgment to himself, not discerning the Lord's body. For this reason many are weak and sick among you, and many sleep. For if we would judge ourselves, we would not be judged. But when we are judged, we are chastened by the Lord, that we may not be condemned with the world. 1 Corinthians 11:29-32

Can sickness sometimes be a result of sin? How? What is the solution for that kind of sickness?

Can sickness sometimes be the result of wrong or unhealthy choices? What is the solution for that kind of sickness? Do you think it is ungodly for a person to allow those choices to continue to affect their body and their life?

3. Search me, O God, and know my heart; try me, and know my anxieties; and see if there is any wicked way in me, and lead me in the way everlasting. Psalm 139:23-24

Do you think we are to judge ourselves? Have you ever searched your own heart and asked God to reveal any areas of unconfessed sin in your life?

4. *...not returning evil for evil or reviling for reviling, but on the contrary blessing, knowing that you were called to this, that you may inherit a blessing. 1 Peter 3:9*

Do you think people are being evil when they say your sickness is due to a lack of faith? Why or why not? If God tells us to respond to evil with blessing, how do you think He wants us to respond to those judging us?

5. *So then, my beloved brethren, let every man be swift to hear, slow to speak, slow to wrath... James 1:19*

Do you find yourself feeling angry and giving a quick response when your faith is questioned? What does this verse tell us about how we should respond?

6. *...for the wrath of man does not produce the righteousness of God. James 1:19-20*

Why is it important that we don't respond in anger? How does anger affect us physically—is it helpful or hurtful? How does it affect us emotionally? Spiritually?

7. Looking carefully lest anyone fall short of the grace of God; lest any root of bitterness springing up cause trouble, and by this many become defiled. Hebrews 12:15

Do we have permission or the right to be bitter even when mistreated? How can bitterness defile not just that person, but many others, too? Due to the long-term negative effects on the body, is God being unkind or kind when He tell us to choose not to be bitter?

Look up this verse and read the verses before and afterward. What is the context? Why were the people in this passage at risk for becoming bitter?

8. Therefore the sisters sent to Him, saying, "Lord, behold, he whom You love is sick."

When Jesus heard that, He said, "This sickness is not unto death, but for the glory of God, that the Son of God may be glorified through it."

Now Jesus loved Martha and her sister and Lazarus. John 11:3-5

If fellow believers had said Mary and Martha's brother was sick because of his lack of faith, or that he died because of theirs, what do you think Jesus would have said in response?

9. Therefore let us, as many as are mature, have this mind; and if in anything you think otherwise, God will reveal even this to you. Philippians 3:15

In the end, is your amount of faith anyone's business but yours and God's? In your opinion, should we let other people be wrong and let God change their hearts, should we try to convince them, or does it depend on the person and situation?

10. Of the following verses, which do you think would be best for you to use with those who doubt your faith?

John 9:2-3

And His disciples asked Him, saying, "Rabbi, who sinned, this man or his parents, that he was born blind?"

Jesus answered, "Neither this man nor his parents sinned, but that the works of God should be revealed in him."

John 16:33

These things I have spoken to you, that in Me you may have peace. In the world you will have tribulation; but be of good cheer, I have overcome the world.

2 Timothy 2:3

You therefore must endure hardship as a good soldier of Jesus Christ.

Other:

(For a more extensive look on health and wealth and how Jesus' actions and words refute it, see *Why Doesn't God Fix It?* Appendix B: *Jesus, Healing, and Faith*)

Notes:

Chapter Four:

Why Didn't Jesus Heal Everybody?

. . . Jesus chose to heal individuals, and sometimes He healed huge masses of people in need, but He knew men's hearts. He knew healing everyone would be an easy ticket to personal fame, but not fulfill the ultimate purpose of His time on earth. Healing was good, but not it if took away from salvation.

Perhaps that is one of the reasons why God has not healed those of us who live with chronic illness. He has a higher purpose than us feeling comfortable and whole again. His gospel is not about health and wealth. Rather, it often requires sacrifice here in this life. If that sacrifice fulfills God's ultimate purpose, is it not better to be sick than to be well? Our choice to honor Him and glorify Him when He doesn't fix it is more testimony to the world than were we all better and back to living life the way we want.

One day all of God's children—every person who has accepted Jesus as Savior—will be healed of everything that binds us in this life. Our time here will seem such a small, insignificant season. In heaven, we will not mind having been sick here on earth, it if meant representing our God well. Living the truth of His power, not just to make the bad go away, but to uphold and strengthen within the bad.

Be comforted in knowing there is purpose in your pain, and share that comfort with others . . .

1. Jesus answered and said to them, "Those who are well have no need of a physician, but those who are sick. I have not come to call the righteous, but sinners, to repentance." Luke 5:31-32

Why did Jesus come to earth? How could healing people help that purpose? Were there times when healing would not help that purpose?

2. And He cast out the spirits with a word, and healed all who were sick, that it might be fulfilled which was spoken by Isaiah the prophet, saying: "He Himself took our infirmities and bore our sicknesses." Matthew 8:16-17

In this passage, Jesus healed everyone who came to Him. Why does the passage say He did that?

3. Jesus answered them and said, "Most assuredly, I say to you, you seek Me, not because you saw the signs, but because you ate of the loaves and were filled. Do not labor for the food which perishes, but for the food which endures to everlasting life, which the Son of Man will give you, because God the Father has set His seal on Him."

····Therefore they said to Him, "What sign will You perform then, that we may see it and believe You? What work will You do? Our fathers ate the manna in the desert; as it is written, 'He gave them bread from heaven to eat.'"

Then Jesus said to them, "Most assuredly, I say to you, Moses did not give you the bread from heaven, but My Father gives you the true bread from heaven. For the bread of God is He who comes down from heaven and gives life to the world."

Then they said to Him, "Lord, give us this bread always."

And Jesus said to them, "I am the bread of life. He who comes to Me shall never hunger, and he who believes in Me shall never thirst."

John 6:26-27,30-35

Jesus preached about spiritual bread and living water (see John 4:7-26), but both times, His hearers asked for bread to quench their current hunger and water to quench their physical thirst. In this same way, would a focus on healing potentially distract from Jesus' message of spiritual deliverance over physical deliverance? Do you see that faulty priority of the physical among believers today?

4. And behold, a leper came and worshiped Him, saying, "Lord, if You are willing, You can make me clean."

Then Jesus put out His hand and touched him, saying, "I am willing; be cleansed." Immediately his leprosy was cleansed.

And Jesus said to him, "See that you tell no one; but go your way, show yourself to the priest, and offer the gift that Moses commanded, as a testimony to them."

Matthew 8:2-4

Jesus could have healed the leper with a word. Instead, He touched him, making Himself ceremonially unclean. Jesus touched the leper when he was still leprous. What do you think this passage teaches us about Jesus? Which aspect do you think is most significant—that the man was healed, that Jesus told him not to tell, or that Jesus touched an untouchable outcast? Why?

5. Then Jesus went about all the cities and villages, teaching in their synagogues, preaching the gospel of the kingdom, and healing every sickness and every disease among the people. Matthew 9:35

This is another passage where Jesus healed everyone. Is it assumed those coming had faith to be healed, or do you think there might have been some unconscious people or non-believing people in the group? Do the verses before or after give weight to your theory?

6. And their eyes were opened. And Jesus sternly warned them, saying, "See that no one knows it." But when they had departed, they spread the news about Him in all that country. Matthew 9:30-31

The two blind men had faith to be healed but not enough faith to obey. Could they have shown their gratitude and spread the name of Jesus without focusing on their physical healing? How? Do you think that is what Jesus would have preferred?

7. Heal the sick, cleanse the lepers, raise the dead, cast out demons. Freely you have received, freely give. Matthew 10:8

Jesus instructed His disciples to freely heal, cast out devils and even raise the dead on their mission. This brings up interesting points, including:

1. Judas was listed in verse four. He was given the ability to heal even though he was a false disciple and Jesus knew it.
2. Jesus told them to freely heal. No mention was made regarding the sick person's level of faith.
3. The healing was in accompaniment to their preaching the kingdom.
4. They were sent to the Jews, the lost sheep of Israel, implying those receiving healing were not yet believers at all.

This passage seems to show that large scale healings were to accompany initial presentations of the gospel as proof that they were genuine prophets of Jehovah. Do other times when Jesus healed many fit that conclusion? What would that mean for "faith healers" who seek large crowds but can't heal everyone who comes?

8. *For He healed many, so that as many as had afflictions pressed about Him to touch Him. And the unclean spirits, whenever they saw Him, fell down before Him and cried out, saying, "You are the Son of God." But He sternly warned them that they should not make Him known. Mark 3:10-12*

Then He healed many who were sick with various diseases, and cast out many demons; and He did not allow the demons to speak, because they knew Him. Mark 1:34

If Jesus preached a kingdom of health and wealth, wouldn't He have allowed the demons to tell others who He was? Instead He silenced the demons and sometimes told healed people not to tell others what He had done. When Satan tempted Him to show He was the Messiah in a big, powerful and obvious way, He refused (Luke 4:9-12). What does this say about Jesus' purpose in ministry compared to men who want huge crowds and lots of number results?

9. *Now He could do no mighty work there, except that He laid His hands on a few sick people and healed them. Mark 6:5*

This passage and many others show that faith is an important part in healing. Not having faith was the reason many were not healed, not a faith that wasn't big enough. Do you think the man's statement, "Lord, I believe. Help my unbelief." is enough faith for a loved one to be healed? Read Mark 9:23-29 for the answer! (Note how the man's faith was the same, but Jesus' disciples were unable to cast the demon out because of their own lack of power, not the man's lack of faith.)

10. "Return to your own house, and tell what great things God has done for you." And he went his way and proclaimed throughout the whole city what great things Jesus had done for him. Luke 8:39

The one person Jesus instructed to go and tell what Jesus had done was a man destroyed by sin. When Jesus freed him from the demons, Jesus gave him his life back, and hope for the future when all hope had been gone. What would hearers likely focus most on about Jesus if hearing this man's account of deliverance? What would people mostly focus on or be drawn to about Jesus if hearing about a healing from sickness? What does this tell us about what our story of deliverance should focus on? How has Christ already delivered us?

Notes:

Chapter Five:

The Annoying Voice Inside My Head

. . . We all need to be just as careful about what we feed out minds as we are about what we feed out bodies. A good rule is the Philippians 4:8 test, which says we should think on things that are true, noble, just, pure, lovely, virtuous, praiseworthy, and of good report. These are the things we are to focus on. That takes purpose.

The little voice in my head is never going to leave for good. But I can tune it out, making that voice smaller as God's voice gains volume. I am going to take those bad thoughts into captivity, reject them, and replace them with what is true and lovely . . .

1. And let the peace of God rule in your hearts, to which also you were called in one body; and be thankful. Colossians 3:15

Why do you think being thankful is a commandment put right after letting the peace of God rule in our hearts? Do you think peace and thankfulness go together? Is being thankful a good antidote for the it's-not-fair feelings? How?

2. Finally, brethren, whatever things are true, whatever things are noble, whatever things are just, whatever things are pure, whatever things are lovely, whatever things are of good report, if there is any virtue and if there is anything praiseworthy— meditate on these things. Philippians 4:8

What are the things that are easy to meditate on? Are those easy things on the list above? Why do you think this list is in the Bible? How can it help corral our thoughts?

3. All things are lawful for me, but not all things are helpful; all things are lawful for me, but not all things edify. 1 Corinthians 10:23

What are some of the thoughts chronically ill people tend to think that are not helpful? What are the consequences of the unhelpful thoughts?

4. And do not be conformed to this world, but be transformed by the renewing of your mind, that you may prove what is that good and acceptable and perfect will of God. Romans 12:2

Do you find on internet groups or in-person groups, it is easy to join in those conversations of complaint? (It's not fair. People don't understand. It's so hard.) What do you see as the world's pattern of thought when it comes to illness? How does God's perspective on illness differ from the world's? Do you think changing from the world's perspective to God's would help us? How do we do that?

5. Casting down arguments and every high thing that exalts itself against the knowledge of God, bringing every thought into captivity to the obedience of Christ. 2 Corinthians 10:5

Ah, here's how we do that! Do you think it is excessive that the verse talks about every thought? Why or why not? How do you personally take thoughts captive? Do you quote Scripture, tell yourself things that are true and lovely, something else? Share and help each other learn more ways to overcome!

The Bible has help for every destructive thought or feeling we encounter. Below, write the feelings or thoughts you struggle with most, then look in God's Word for a verse to memorize, to quote when attacked. Here are a few to start with:

Feeling - Replacement Truth	Verses to Memorize
Anxiety - Peace	Do not be anxious about anything, but... (Phil. 4:6)
	Casting all your anxiety on him...(I Pet.5:7)
Self-Pity - Contentment/Gratitude	
Despair - Hope	
Envy/Anger/Bitterness - Grace/Love	
Giving Up - Endurance	
Suffering - Joy	

Notes:

Chapter Six:

God I'll Trust You If . . .

. . . There's a boundary line somewhere in my soul. Anything within that boundary, I can trust God with. But the closer circumstances get to that boundary line, or especially if they cross it, that's too far. Too risky. Too much. I stop trusting God and start asking (whining, pleading, begging) Him to change the circumstances until they are back within the boundary of my ability to trust Him.

God wants us to have no boundaries when it comes to trusting Him. It is impossible to do so, humanly speaking. It is impossible to trust God with the impossible, with the truly frightening, with the incomprehensible.

And yet, God reaches to us where we are and nudges us toward those boundaries of trust. He asks us to cross the line. He leads us to walk with Him through the unanswered questions, allowing Him to replace our fears with a peace that doesn't make any sense (Phil. 4:7) . . .

1. I will both lie down in peace, and sleep; for You alone, O LORD, make me dwell in safety. Psalm 4:8

Are some parts of our lives easy to trust God with? What parts are hard to trust God with? Why do you think these parts are harder? Why do you think it is so hard to trust God with everything?

2. Whenever I am afraid, I will trust in You. Psalm 56:3

What are you afraid of when it comes to your health? What thoughts come to mind along with the fear? Do you think this verse talks about a feeling or a choice, or both? Elaborate.

3. Trust in Him at all times, you people; pour out your heart before Him; God is a refuge for us. Psalm 62:8

Do you pour out your heart before God? Do you tell Him what you truly fear? Why or why not? Do you think Christians in general are open about their fears, or is that a taboo subject? Why? Do you think fears are a taboo subject with God?

4. The LORD your God in your midst, the Mighty One, will save; He will rejoice over you with gladness, He will quiet you with His love, He will rejoice over you with singing." Zephaniah 3:17

Does this verse surprise you, to think of God Himself singing over you? When do people tend to sing over other people? Do we sing over people we are disappointed in or frustrated with? How do you most often feel when you sing over someone? Can you imagine God feeling that way about you? Does that change how you feel about trusting Him with your deepest fears?

The verse also talks about God being the Mighty One. Does knowing God can do anything help you trust Him more, or just bring up more questions? Explain.

Look up the following verses. Highlight in your Bible those meaningful to you, and write below those you want to memorize for your fight against fear.

Fear of Death   1 Corinthians 15:54, Psalm 23

Fear of Pain   Revelation 21:4, Isaiah 66:13

Fear of Long-Term Illness   James 1:12, James 5:11

Fear of Aging   2 Corinthians 4:16

Fear of Criticism   Psalm 62:8, Matthew 5:11

Fear of Failure   Proverbs 24:16, Psalm 37:24

Fear of Loss   Revelation 21:4, 1 Thessalonians 4:13

Fear of being Forgotten or Rejected by others   Psalm 27:10, Zephaniah 3:17

Fear of being Forgotten or Rejected by God   Romans 8:35-39, Jeremiah 31:3

What fears and verses can you add to the list?

Notes:

Chapter Seven:

Illness and Depression

. . . Whether you are genetically inclined toward depression, personality inclined toward depression, or you've never even come close to depression, the truth is that now, with chronic health problems, it is something you need to be prepared to battle. We must learn to live according to the truth, not our feelings. For the truth sets us free.

How did I get past the fear of depression taking over again? I learned during that pregnancy time to fight the feelings not by focusing on them, but by focusing on truth. From the moment I woke, I turned my mind away from those thoughts (I did not start analyzing them but rejected them, like mentally flushing a toilet) and instead quoted Scripture, as I got up and went to the bathroom, until I was back in bed. It was the only thing powerful enough to cover over and replace the dark thoughts.

God's Word is powerful enough to fight any feeling. I do not have to be controlled by my emotions anymore. I have the truth, and the truth has set me free.

It can set you free, too . . .

1. For God has not given us a spirit of fear, but of power and of love and of a sound mind. 2 Timothy 1:7

Have you ever thought that feelings of fear came from God? Do you think a *moment* of fear, such as if you're in the road and a truck is coming, is a God-given fear? Do you think *seasons* of fear, like depression, are God-given? Why or why not?

2. Therefore let us pursue the things which make for peace and the things by which one may edify another. Romans 14:19

In your opinion, is it possible to be at peace when depressed? Why or why not? Why do you think God commands here not just to be at peace, but to pursue the things that result in peace? Do you think peace is something you have to work at?

3. He also brought me up out of a horrible pit, out of the miry clay, and set my feet upon a rock, and established my steps. Psalm 40:2

Please share your own experiences with depression and how God got you out of that pit. What resources helped? What verses helped? Have you ever written down or recorded those helpful things as ammunition for the next time you battle depression?

4. We are hard-pressed on every side, yet not crushed; we are perplexed, but not in despair; persecuted, but not forsaken; struck down, but not destroyed—always carrying about in the body the dying of the Lord Jesus, that the life of Jesus also may be manifested in our body.

Do you feel like the first half of this verse describes you right now? The second part of the verse almost seems like it doesn't fit. How can carrying about Jesus' suffering help us with our own? What do you think this verse means?

Does this verse give comfort, knowing that no matter how close to the edge you feel, there is hope? You may be hard-pressed and perplexed and even persecuted, but you do not have to be crushed or in despair, and you are definitely not forsaken!

5. Bear one another's burdens, and so fulfill the law of Christ. Galatians 6:2

Does this verse give you permission to keep your fears and struggles to yourself? How can God's people follow this commandment if they do not know each other's burdens?

Why do you think we are inclined to hide away when we struggle and not be open? How do you think people would respond if we told them what was really going on?

6. Let each of you look out not only for his own interests, but also for the interests of others. Philippians 2:4

Depression eats away at a person and keeps them hidden inside themselves. Looking at the above two verses, is it ever okay for a Christian to hide away? How can depression keep a person from honoring God in this matter?

7. *The generous soul will be made rich, and he who waters will also be watered himself. Proverbs 11:25*

As difficult as it is at the time, does getting the focus off ourselves and onto others help with depression? If you think no, why not? If you think yes, how? What does this verse promise us if we choose to make the effort to invest in other people despite how we feel? Does generosity only apply to money?

8. *Hear my cry, O God; attend to my prayer. From the end of the earth I will cry to You, when my heart is overwhelmed; lead me to the rock that is higher than I. Psalm 61:1-2*

When we feel overwhelmed, what should we do? Is there a way mentioned in this verse to get above ourselves—the power of our feelings—and be safe?

9. For You have been a shelter for me, a strong tower from the enemy. I will abide in Your tabernacle forever; I will trust in the shelter of Your wings. Psalm 61:3-4

Birds protect their young by sheltering them under their wings. God uses this characteristic to represent Himself with His children many times. How can we find rest in the shelter of His wings? What does that mean in everyday life? Why can we trust Him there?

It is interesting that running away from our problems by hiding inside ourselves is destructive and fearful, but if we run to God and hide there, we find rest and peace. What do you think about the idea of running away being a good thing or bad thing depending on where we run?

10. My flesh and my heart fail; but God is the strength of my heart and my portion forever. Psalm 73:26

This verse is beautiful. Even if our hearts and our bodies feel like they're falling apart, God strengthens our failing hearts and provides for us. Forever. How can we live this verse this week?

Notes:

Chapter Eight:

The If Onlys and What Ifs

. . . Most of us have officially declared Jesus Christ our Savior. We have asked Him to forgive our sins and give us heaven.

But when it comes to handing over our lives, our days, our present circumstances and yes, even our health, we may have never actually handed those over to Him. (Or, if you're like me, you have the bad habit of taking them back to worry over them again!) We say we trust God, but most of the time we say that when things are in control.

Do we really trust God? Enough to believe that even our health problems are part of His great purpose? Enough to stop complaining about them as some random thing that happened to us, and see them as a useful tool in God's kingdom? Enough to choose peace in the midst of pain?

That is a very hard thing to do. It's even harder when we are thinking on the What Ifs and If Onlys. And we can make it even more difficult when our habits and choices keep us walking on the What If and If Only path . . .

1. Not that I have already attained, or am already perfected; but I press on, that I may lay hold of that for which Christ Jesus has also laid hold of me. Philippians 3:12

What has Jesus already "laid hold of" for you? How can your pressing on lay hold of those things? Why do you think we have to be involved in this, instead of it just happening because Jesus has provided it?

2. Brethren, I do not count myself to have apprehended; but one thing I do, forgetting those things which are behind and reaching forward to those things which are ahead, I press toward the goal for the prize of the upward call of God in Christ Jesus. Philippians 3:13-14

Do you feel like you had "apprehended" before your illness and now you've gone backward? Do you think perhaps you've looked at the past with a slightly unrealistic perspective? Is it possible to start focusing on here and forward instead of the past? Why is that difficult? What do you think the benefit would be?

3. As far as the east is from the west, so far has He removed our transgressions from us. Psalm 103:12

If for you, looking back includes sorrow and shame, what do you need to do to be able to leave the past behind? Confess sin (1 John 1:9), or change an ungodly habit (Proverbs 26:11)?

4. Rejoice in the Lord always. Again I will say, rejoice! Philippians 4:4

Is it possible to obey this command while concentrating on the If Onlys and What Ifs? Why or why not?

5. Not that I speak in regard to need, for I have learned in whatever state I am, to be content. Philippians 4:11

We tend to think of contentment as a feeling. Why then do you think Paul said he had "learned" to be content? Can contentment be a skill it is possible to develop?

Do you know any content people? Are they content because everything in their life is easy and comfortable? What do you think they choose to focus on that gives them contentment?

6. I know how to be abased, and I know how to abound. Everywhere and in all things I have learned both to be full and to be hungry, both to abound and to suffer need. Philippians 4:12

Do you think it matters who we spend our time with? If we choose friends who have learned contentment, is it easier to be content than if we spend time with people living in the If Onlys and What Ifs? How do our associations affect our own thoughts, conversations, and actions?

With chronic illness, life can change day by day, abounding one day and abasing us the next. Does this verse tell us we can be joyful on the good days and have a right to grouch on the bad days? If Paul was writing this directly to people with chronic illness, what do you think he would say?

7. I can do all things through Christ who strengthens me. Philippians 4:13

Most believers know this verse. It is quoted often, but minus the previous verses that explain why this verse is needed. What are the trials listed in the verses previous that let us know this is no fluffy statement? What are the "all things" Paul needs Christ's strength to do, based on your knowledge of his life and the above Scriptures? Do you find similarities to your own life?

Do you believe Christ is really strong enough to give you contentment through all your trials? Why or why not?

8. Cast your burden on the LORD, and He shall sustain you. Psalm 55:22

What is the requirement for being sustained? Why do we want to hold on to our burdens instead of casting them onto the Lord? What is the burden you cling to most?

9. Open your mouth wide, and I will fill it. Psalm 81:10

Do you think our level of contentment and joy is our own choice? Would choosing to leave the past behind and live where we are help us move forward with joy?

God says He will fill us. What is the requirement for that listed in this verse? That seems a given, but in our lives, if we refuse to be glad where we are, can God give us joy in our lives now?

10. In everything give thanks; for this is the will of God in Christ Jesus for you. 1 Thessalonians 5:18

What is the will of God for you in this current season of your life? When is it easy to give thanks? When is it hard? Do you think there is a reason for God saying to give thanks *in* everything as opposed to giving thanks *for* everything? Explain.

What can you give thanks for right now?

(If you can't think of anything, look up these verses: Eph. 1:6, Jer. 29:11, Luke 10:20, 2 Pet. 1:3, Phil. 4:19, Matt. 28:20)

Notes:

Chapter Nine:

Hurting Alone

. . . I do not presume to have a magic formula to fix this. I'm not going to tell you to just focus on happy things and get over it, or burden you further by saying you should get out more and find a bunch of friends. No, sometimes there is no easy solution. Sometimes the pain is not the absence of loved ones, but rather their rejection, and that is a wound not quickly healed.

The only thing I can offer is a loved one who never falters for a moment in His love for you. Yes, I'm talking about God. No, I'm not offering a pat answer, a way to ignore your pain. Exactly the opposite. I have learned that the deeper the pain, the more only God can be the answer. Only He truly understands. Only He knows how deep our suffering penetrates.

And yet He, the one who knows our darkest moments of despair, our worst feelings of anger, our biggest temptations to bitterness; He is the one who loves us most . . .

1. God is our refuge and strength, a very present help in trouble. Therefore we will not fear, even though the earth be removed, and though the mountains be carried into the midst of the sea; though its waters roar and be troubled, though the mountains shake with its swelling. Psalm 46:2-3

This passage lists some very fearful things. Why does it say we will not fear despite there being plenty to fear? Do you think that is a significant reason? Why is there such power in God's presence?

2. Can a woman forget her nursing child, and not have compassion on the son of her womb? Surely they may forget, yet I will not forget you. See, I have inscribed you on the palms of My hands; your walls are continually before Me. Isaiah 49:15-16

Do you think God cares about our pain? Does He hurt with us when we hurt? Why or why not? Does this passage present a different view of God than you usually picture? Have you ever thought of God as being like a mother? Why or why not?

3. And we know that all things work together for good to those who love God, to those who are the called according to His purpose. Romans 8:28

This is a commonly quoted verse, but people like to leave out the ending. It does not say God will work out things for good for everyone. Who does He work things out for good for? Why do you think that stipulation is put in? What does it mean for us?

4. Let your conduct be without covetousness; be content with such things as you have. For He Himself has said, "I will never leave you nor forsake you." Hebrews 13:5

Are you tempted to covet other people's good health, level of energy, lack of problems? This verse doesn't say we shouldn't covet because it's wrong or because it will make us miserable. Why does the verse say we shouldn't covet? How do God's words here help us to be content even with sickness or pain?

If we are God's we are never truly alone. List or discuss the times you feel most alone. Where can you put this verse to remind you of God's presence during those times?

5. When my father and my mother forsake me, then the LORD will take care of me. Psalm 27:10

Do you think this verse is just for children? Does it also apply to grown children? Could it apply about spouses and siblings and other friends and relatives as well? Do you think we can really turn to God as we would like to turn to family and friends? What is harder about turning to God alone? What is better about turning to God alone?

6. The LORD is near to those who have a broken heart. Psalm 38:14

Does this verse speak to you? How would you visualize these words? If you knew someone who was brokenhearted, how would you comfort them? Can you see God comforting you that way? Why or why not?

7. Yea, though I walk through the valley of the shadow of death, I will fear no evil; for You are with me. Psalm 23:4

Again, what is the reason not to fear? Is the reason to fear legitimate? Do you sometimes feel your situation is more serious than others believe it to be? Do you think God recognizes the true level of difficulty? Does it help to know He knows the reality, no matter what anyone else may think?

8. The LORD is good, a stronghold in the day of trouble; and He knows those who trust in Him. Nahum 1:7

What do you think of when you hear the word "stronghold"? Do you have a place where you feel safe and free? Does going to God feel like going to that place? Why or why not? Do you think if you looked to God to fill and comfort you, would your need to look to others lessen? Would then the hurt at others' rejection lesson as well?

9. What then shall we say to these things? If God is for us, who can be against us? He who did not spare His own Son, but delivered Him up for us all, how shall He not with Him also freely give us all things?

Who shall bring a charge against God's elect? It is God who justifies. Who is he who condemns? It is Christ who died, and furthermore is also risen, who is even at the right hand of God, who also makes intercession for us. Romans 8:31-34

How do these verses speak to you about those who would say you're faking it, or you're worth less because you can do less, or you should just do _____ and you'll feel better?

10. Who shall separate us from the love of Christ? Shall tribulation, or distress, or persecution, or famine, or nakedness, or peril, or sword? As it is written:

"For Your sake we are killed all day long; we are accounted as sheep for the slaughter."

Yet in all these things we are more than conquerors through Him who loved us. For I am persuaded that neither death nor life, nor angels nor principalities nor powers, nor things present nor things to come, nor height nor depth, nor any other created thing, shall be able to separate us from the love of God which is in Christ Jesus our Lord. Romans 8:35-39

Have you ever considered that the One who loves you most is also the One who says nothing—NOTHING—can separate you from His love? Does it give comfort to know that God's love for you will never change, no matter what? It can be so discouraging knowing others judge us or don't believe us or reject us because of our ongoing illness and the problems it causes. How can these verses give us a value no amount of illness can take away?

Notes:

Chapter Ten:

When the Mountain Won't Move

. . . For some of us, God wants the mountain to remain. Moving it might impress people and make them feel like we have faith, but sometimes it takes more faith to let God be glorified through our suffering rather than being delivered from it.

As in Hebrews, sometimes God is glorified by delivering His children from the trial. Other times, He is glorified by helping them endure it. God has a purpose for each of us individually, and trying to decide why one was delivered from, and another is being delivered through, is faulty. As Paul warns in 2 Corinthians 10:12, "But they, measuring themselves by themselves, and comparing themselves among themselves, are not wise."

Sometimes it takes more faith to not get what we want. That kind shows, but it's a lot like beauty. Sometimes we see someone who is beautiful, but we can't pinpoint it to their lips or eyes or the shape of their nose, or any one feature. (I don't think I've ever seen a beautiful nose, now that I think about it.) They just shine. That's the kind of faith we who live with illness can have. The kind that looks up and is radiant and unashamed (Psalm 34:5). The kind that, like the mountains, others can look to and be comforted . . .

1. Read the entire chapter of Hebrews 11. List some of the wonderful things the people of faith received.

Now list some of the things you noticed that did not look like things people of great faith should experience. Can you find any person in this chapter who lived a life of health and wealth?

2. Now faith is the substance of things hoped for, the evidence of things not seen. Hebrews 11:1

How does this verse argue against faith always producing visible results?

3. These all died in faith, not having received the promises, but having seen them afar off were assured of them, embraced them and confessed that they were strangers and pilgrims on the earth. Hebrews 11:13

Health and wealth teaches that faith gets you the promises now. What do these verses teach? Was their faith based on immediate visible results, or is there more to faith than current circumstances being fixed? For those with chronic illness, if we were to receive perfect health right now, do you think we would feel as strongly that we are "strangers and pilgrims on the earth"? Why or why not?

4. But now they desire a better, that is, a heavenly country. Therefore God is not ashamed to be called their God, for He has prepared a city for them. Hebrews 11:16

Why was God "not ashamed to be called their God"? How can chronic illness help us desire a better country?

5. Others were tortured, not accepting deliverance, that they might obtain a better resurrection....They were stoned, they were sawn in two, were tempted, were slain with the sword. They wandered about in sheepskins and goatskins, being destitute, afflicted, tormented— of whom the world was not worthy. Hebrews 11: 35b, 37, 38a

Is there ever a time when our immediate healing should not be the highest goal? What might be more important than our comfort in this life?

6. Therefore we also, since we are surrounded by so great a cloud of witnesses, let us lay aside every weight, and the sin which so easily ensnares us, and let us run with endurance the race that is set before us. Hebrews 12:1

Knowing the heroes of chapter 11 are looking on, how can their faith motivate us to run our race with patience?

7. Looking unto Jesus, the author and finisher of our faith, who for the joy that was set before Him endured the cross, despising the shame, and has sat down at the right hand of the throne of God. For consider Him who endured such hostility from sinners against Himself, lest you become weary and discouraged in your souls. Hebrews 12:2-3

Who is our ultimate example of faith to follow? Why Jesus instead of someone living comfortably here and now?

8. But without faith it is impossible to please Him, for he who comes to God must believe that He is, and that He is a rewarder of those who diligently seek Him. Hebrews 11:6

In the end, should faith be about pleasing us or pleasing God? Does this verse imply that we are rewarded or not based on the amount of our faith, or something else?

9. "Father, if it is Your will, take this cup away from Me; nevertheless not My will, but Yours, be done." Luke 22:42

Can we follow Jesus' example in His prayers by wanting God's will more than our own? Do you think such a commitment would need to be more a choice or a feeling?

10. I will lift up my eyes to the hills—from whence comes my help? My help comes from the L*ORD, Who made heaven and earth. Psalm 121:1-2*

Now at the end of this book, how will you choose to see your mountains? Where will you get your help from?

Notes:

But we have this treasure

in earthen vessels,

that the excellence of the power

may be of God and not of us.

We are hard-pressed on every side,

yet not crushed;

we are perplexed,

but not in despair;

persecuted, but not forsaken;

struck down,

but not destroyed.

2 Corinthians 4:7-9

ABOUT THE AUTHOR

Kimberly Rae has Addison's disease, hypoglycemia, asthma, scoliosis, and a cyst on her brain. She has been published over 300 times and writes regularly on living joyfully despite chronic illness. Her Christian suspense/romance novels on international human trafficking (*Stolen Woman, Stolen Child,* and *Stolen Future*) are all Amazon bestsellers.

Rae has lived in Bangladesh, Uganda, Kosovo and Indonesia. She now lives in the foothills of the Blue Ridge Mountains in North Carolina with her husband and two children.

Find more books in the series or contact the author at
www.kimberlyrae.com.

Made in the USA
Lexington, KY
28 September 2015